OPEN YOUR EARS

OPEN YOUR EARS

THINGS TO KNOW ABOUT BUSINESS NO ONE WILL EVER TELL YOU

THOMAS BULOW

ISBN-13: 978-1-942389-12-5

Prominent Books

Published by Prominent Books, LLC.

Prominent Books and the Prominent Books logo are property of Prominent Books, LLC.

TABLE OF CONTENTS

DEDICATION

I want to thank you, Barb, for your support, patience and understanding. I would not have made it at work without you. Fourteen-hour days didn't leave a whole lot of time to be home. You did an amazing job raising our kids too. Together, we made it all work.

ACKNOWLEDGMENTS

I'd like to acknowledge a lot of people but know I'd forget somebody, which wouldn't be okay. So I'll pair down my list to just these few. Just know that I will never forget anyone who has helped or supported me along the way.

Joe Basic, my dad and my wife were big inspirations to me at different levels and in different ways.

Bill Crowhurst—The Electrical Genius—taught me many tricks of the trade.

Greg Zawaski always gave invaluable credit intel on companies I considered getting involved with.

Mr. Cachey, Mr. Febbel and Mr. Turcich were the three true gentlemen who inspired me to try to be like them.

Special Note

I would like you to have the information that was shared with me by some very smart people, and a few things I learned the hard way.

I think I was lucky to be at the right place, right time when these individuals bothered to set me straight on things I was clueless about.

Without the great employees, accountants and attorneys, nothing would have been possible.

Also, I hope that you pass on this information to others.

1

A LIFETIME OF LEARNING THE HARD WAY

This book allows me to pass on things that took me a long time to learn. I have been fortunate to meet some amazing people in my life—many through my electrical business. For whatever reason, they saw fit to share their life and business lessons with me. They made me laugh, humbled me, and most importantly, they helped me to become wiser. Many shared some great stories that helped positively influence me. I want to share these stories, along with my own, in this book.

I started in business when I was 22 years old. I bought part of a company, Palos Electric. It had no money. Starting out in the trenches made me a better person for life and business.

There are no do-overs, and nobody is going to come to your rescue like when you were young. As a kid, you are protected. But you will quickly grow up and have to face the world on your own. That is real life. The pre-adult stint is supposed to include education on how to make a success of your life, your family, your work, your country, and your world. They are all connected.

The sad fact is you are not being shown how to succeed in life. You are being shown how to conform, comply, and support someone else's ideals.

There is no education I have ever seen regarding how to make it in this dog-eat-dog world. You are just thrown into the freezing cold water, or just thrown to the wolves. However you want to describe the shock of coming of age, it is not a slow process.

Some people just have to work their butts off to make a single thing happen. You will learn in this book that the easy route makes you weak. How fortunate is anyone who has no idea what their limits are? With Daddy's money, you will never know the uncertainty of tomorrow.

Although life and success are hard as hell, I wouldn't change a thing. Entitled people are often weak in strength and fortitude because they have never had to take the opportunity that is risk. They've never been given the opportunity to risk what is earned from sweating their own sweat and bleeding their own blood.

The things I've learned when under pressure can't be taught. They have to be experienced. The strength that comes from determination can only be achieved by putting everything on the line and taking a shot.

I got up every morning, got my ass kicked, and got up again the next morning for the same beating. After a while, things began to become predictable and all too obvious until one day, I started avoiding a few punches and racked up some points on the scoreboard. Then we started winning more and more.

I was fortunate to have met a lot of incredible individuals who shared their wisdom with me. I might not be a scholar, but I thank my lucky stars I was smart enough to shut my trap and open my ears when these guys took the time from their busy lives to say something profound to me. To me!

I won't just be the bald guy in the corner or a nebulous figure with the names grandpa and great grandpa. What I've learned is priceless, and it would be a shame to lose it all when I'm gone. It should be passed on from generation to generation.

Life is tough, and there is no sugarcoating in this book. I don't take drugs or get into trouble with the police or the IRS, but I am a smart ass. Be prepared for some colorful thoughts and words.

So read this book from cover to cover, and refer back to it whenever you have difficulty. You're not going to find this kind of information in a textbook or classroom.

Is There More to Learn Even for You?

I'd like to make a quick note to those of you who have already seen success in your lives.

No doubt, you know a lot. Because you're successful, it's pretty clear you've got abilities few people have, and you know things most people don't. Sometimes it's a different take on things. Other times it's something completely foreign, unbelievable, or truly eye-opening.

I'm sure there are things I could learn from you. In fact,

you're probably accustomed to giving advice to others, and most of what you hear is old news. I'm just as sure that you still have room to learn a few more valuable things that you can take to the bank. Mathematics alone gives good odds for that. The possibility of you knowing absolutely everything there is to know is ... well, you get the point.

However successful you may be, I'd like to ask you to stop thinking about using this book as a fly swatter and give it a chance. I'm just going to tell you like it is.

2

A Tough Place

If you've ever tried to make something happen that was important to you, then you know all too well that the world is a tough place to live. Life is challenging, and succeeding at anything is *not* easy. Things can quickly begin to look impossible.

Don't think that I'm being pessimistic here. I'm a pretty happy guy, all things considered. I've made something of my life and done some things I'm proud of. I'm not perfect or a saint, but I have a business that stands on its own, employees who make a great living, a marriage that has remained intact, good kids, and a few choice friends who stick around if "you know what" should ever hit the fan. I'm not being cynical, I'm just stating the obvious. The truth isn't often pretty.

The intention behind this book is to provide encouragement in a different way.

No one actually ever fails. People grow tired of not reaching their goals and eventually let go of their dreams.

The fact is, there's a scarcity of valid information on how to succeed. There's too much BS and hype and not enough practical information.

This book is about how to fail as much as it is how to succeed. If you only know what is working for you, and you aren't aware of what is opposing your goals, that's not a good spot to be in.

Succeeding at something, making something of your life, doesn't need to be an overwhelming struggle or impossible. Sometimes it can feel that way when something keeps holding you back and you can't figure out what it is. If you carry this worry long enough, it will start to feel heavier. It will wear on you.

But don't cheat. Honest people succeed all the time. In fact, most people are honest and have good intentions.

3
EDUCATION

The challenge with being successful isn't just a lack of information; it's also getting bad information.

People who tell you it's all simple and easy are trying to sell you something. They're probably not bad people—let's take the high road—but they are trying to sell you something. They sure as hell aren't selling truth because truth isn't glamorous. Few people talk about the pain and suffering of becoming an Olympic athlete. You hear about the glory of winning the gold and representing your country. For obvious reasons, people only want to sell the sparkle and fanfare—show people how it's going to be when they become a millionaire, drive fast cars and live in mansions.

Although people may have good intentions and want to honestly help others succeed, their tactics of only selling the "fun" ... only selling the outcome causes more harm than good. This isn't opinion. Talk to any expert out there, and they will openly admit that only about 18 percent—at best—of their customers ever finish what they start. Even fewer (three percent of the 18) ever reach the heights that were boasted about.

This isn't only in the sales part of their programs. I've yet to see a training program where the teacher was upfront about what it's really going to take to make a success of things. They make a quick mention of something like, "You have to get into action."

Some people promote the desirable "work less" approach to success. It is hard to follow that advice, and often you will end up working harder than most people. Expecting "easy" when it isn't easy is part of the problem.

I'm not on a campaign to bash anyone. Many training programs are the real deal. They just happen to offer a good example of what we see too often in regard to the educational part of success—millionaires selling the glam and glitter, not being completely forthright about how much work it takes to reach their level. Though they mean well, they're creating a new problem. People get the idea they have credible information when it is in fact false or misleading.

There's plenty of "rah-rah" and "let's go get 'em!" which has its place, but why so much sugarcoating? Do successful people really think that low of their audience to feel they need to hold back the hardcore truth? Are people *that* fragile?

You may be starting to realize this isn't a feel-good book. You can get your "attaboys!" and pats on the back from your coach, a motivational book or wherever you can find it. There's plenty of it going around. That's all good and has its place, but this book is going to stick with straight talk. There is too *little* of that going around. It's a bit backwards, but the things you need to hear are the hardest to find.

What Are You?

People can describe others in creative ways. If you're a competitor, you're probably going to be called unfavorable things. Whether they're true or not doesn't matter. What's important is that you don't let it get to you.

I'm not highly educated; I'm self-taught and street smart. This kind of knowledge is obtained the hard way. You get up in the morning, get your butt whipped and do it again the next day. That's one tough way to learn, but, boy, do you learn! Out of necessity—or desperation—you *never* want to experience what just happened ever again.

And when push comes to shove, no one with a textbook is going to ever beat a man with a mission. In other words, don't bring a book to a gunfight. Another way to put it is, don't bring your diploma to work. Bring your tools, and be ready to get your hands dirty.

Professors Try to Teach in the Classroom, But Business is Learned in the Trenches

Professors cover the basics and the ABCs of business, but they don't teach what counts. Nine out of ten of them have never run a business. They went to school to learn what they are now teaching, which can be useless in day-to-day business.

These professors are not going to be able to teach real business to kids. They are going to bring up certain aspects and textbook scenarios that don't adequately show how to get out of hot water or set up operations in the real world. How are you going to meet payroll? How are you going to generate money? How are you going to promote what you do? How are you going to save money on materials? How are you going to do any of this? Give me some nuts and bolts that prepare me for anything, and I'll add more zeros to my paycheck.

Experience makes you smart, at least in most areas of life that count. The arrogant idea of believing that all you need to know is from books shuts down the possibility of ever learning what really matters. Using hands-on experience allows you to make things happen.

What makes the individual lessons so much more powerful is the accumulation of lessons with your own experiences.

As I'm in my early 60s, I think about how much I now know. Of course, so much is from the pain and suffering of failure. I will never forget how much I have learned from being humble: schlepping the trash out to the curb, making mistakes and owning up to them. Getting in there and doing what your crew is doing, right alongside them, keeps things real and down to earth.

Success can make a real jerk out of you if you don't pay attention. You can become very nearsighted and dumb as hell. Everything you've learned can suddenly go out the window. Spending on things you don't need, thinking you're better than the next guy … and that false sense of being superhuman can do you in. Why? Because you might be able to put on your expensive cape, but you ain't gonna fly or run faster than a speeding train. One day, if you're lucky, you come to realize what an idiot you've been and that you bleed just like everybody else.

The only way you can treat people decently is to treat

them as important as yourself. This is how you retain employees. Oh sure, you give them a hard time if they're slacking off or late, but when the important times come around, they know you've got their backs.

I'm at a point in my life where I want to share what I've learned. I hate the idea of eventually going to my grave with these life and business lessons—they are my Golden Rules. Documenting them continues to put them to good use.

I may joke around in this book and be a wise guy, but don't let that lessen the importance of what I'm sharing. Part of it *is* funny. Part may be considered sarcastic, even downright rude sometimes. So is life. You have to take things with a grain of salt—every now and again make fun of the things that really tick you off.

For the most part, what excites me about this book is what your teacher didn't teach you, your parents didn't tell you, and your business guru doesn't know. Why? This information was never all in one place. It has come from a lot of individuals as well as my own realizations every time I lost, fell or bled.

The main message is this:

Now, more than ever, you have the greatest opportunity to be very successful.

You see, along with the Golden Rules, I share stories (anecdotes) of how people have made millions or lost everything, with the reasons why. By the end of this book, you're going to be one of the "smartest dumb asses" in the world. Let others call you what they will. Don't worry about them. Just get on with your goals and plans.

4

BUSINESS

It's good to have someone who inspires you. They are all that you want to be. The people I idolize are Elon Musk and Henry Ford. They risked it all and didn't care what people thought. These people had what it took.

Are You Really an Entrepreneur?

If the divorce rate weren't bad enough, the failure rate of businesses is astronomical. It might even seem unnatural that close to 90% of all businesses fail. With a broader look on life in general, failure—which can be defined as not making dreams come true—is all too common. Most people reach the end of their lives with major regrets. As hokey and commercial as it might sound, everybody dreams of something better. It's just the question of who does what it takes to bring a vision into something physical. In other words, who can make something out of nothing.

So many people call themselves entrepreneurs for the simple fact that they have a business license, a website or brick-and-mortar location.

Owning a business is very different from *making* one.

Just like respect, honor and trust, no one can simply buy their way into having anything; it has to stand the test of time. Anything worthwhile has to be *earned*. It has to be developed, and it has to continue to evolve.

Some people see water come out of a faucet. They assume it's simple and easy. The entrepreneur sees all that goes on behind the scenes to make a single drop of water come out of the faucet. There's an entire infrastructure of materials, labor and knowledge of how water gets from the reservoir to your kitchen sink. Just imagine the complexity of allowing people to drink the water without getting dysentery!

There is No Easy Way to Succeed

If you're looking to avoid hard work, you're standing in the wrong line. It's as ridiculous as a weightlifter trying to avoid lifting because it's hard to do. Hard work is what it takes to make something from nothing.

Even if you are digging ditches, you have your intentions right and your mind set, you know this "lowly" job is going to one day get you to where you want to be. It won't be a miserable, forced experience.

There's something really basic about wanting to avoid work. If it's something you're trying to avoid, it likely means you aren't passionate about it. It doesn't mean enough for you to enter a zone of discomfort and stay there day after day.

You have to invest a lot of time into your endeavor. This means a lot of sacrifice; missing out on what your friends are doing, not being able to go to the party because you have to get up at 5 a.m.

What's interesting is there's a sliding scale that changes as you continue over time. In the beginning, you work like a dog and see very little return. More sacrifice than pleasure. As you keep going, this starts to move further and further towards success.

I'm toying with you here, but the point is that the harder you work now, the less you will have to work later in your life. If you screw around and do things halfway and just get by, you will never see any shift in the sliding scale of success. You'll just keep teetering in the middle.

When you start in business, it's easier to make money (profit) because you have less overhead. You are doing most of the work. Making money and spending it is easy. Hanging on to it is the tricky part. Once you've been in business for a number of years, you don't want to make a big mistake because you have less time to make up for it.

We always see some moron cruising on a yacht with semi-naked girls dancing all around. This is Hollywood's version of how to succeed. "Success is fun!" No ... it's not! It sucks. You have to work your butt off day in, day out to make something work. The "fun" comes later.

5

Three Steps

Three steps to a successful business: make it, spend it, keep it.

Make It

Know Your Limits

You have to know your limits in business. In most cases, bigger is not better. You want to make the most money you can with the least overhead without going to another level. Limit yourself to the size of jobs you do so your exposure is less. If you did a $20,000,000 job, your exposure to mishap or failure is heavier than if you did a $100,000 job. If you do a bunch of $100,000 jobs, it can add up to the $20,000,000. If one of those jobs goes south, it is not as bad as the $20,000,000 job going south. You would be done, you're out. The $100,000 jobs only take one or two men. The big jobs may have 100 to 250 guys. I know a lot of guys who went out. The percentage of profit is 4-5 times more on the $100,000 jobs than on the big jobs. Big jobs work 2-3 points, and you are working at 10-15 points. The reason is the larger jobs are going to want significantly deeper discounts.

Your gut will tell you when you shouldn't get into something. I know when I am bidding on something out of my realm, and we back off it. People will tell you to live outside of your comfort zone, but maxims never apply across the board. There is a pace with which any business should expand. You will know what it is in your gut, but as a rule of thumb, 15 to 20 percent per year is a sensible growth rate.

Do What You Know You Can Do

Our forte is that we get the job done. Part of that is knowing whether to accept a job or decline it. When we are looking at a job, it comes down to this: can we do it? Do we have the money? Do we have the people with the right skill sets? Do we have the right equipment?

Capital

If you are undercapitalized, you are not going to make it. Know what your costs and overhead are. What happens is you are always behind the eight ball. You are taking work and not making money on it, but you are taking enough to pay your bills. At the end of the day, you owe more than what you have coming in. You are not starting with enough money. Take your receivables, and divide it by the number of employees. That will tell you how much you have per guy. If you are going to add two or three new guys, you have to make sure you have enough coin to do it. Undercapitalization and overhead are the biggest killers of any company.

Theft

It's a big mistake to hire a Purchasing Agent if your company makes large purchases. It is all common sense. It opens the door for theft. For example, if the PA goes to lunch with a vendor/supplier, he could start to become soft and give favors, which would come out of your pocket. In other words, one pal is going to help the other on your dime. You can't take anything from them because they're doing it for that very reason.

Company Evaluation

Don't bother to ever have your company evaluated. It will show a false statement of what it is worth. I learned that it is not what they say it is worth when you try to sell your business. Your business is worth what someone is willing to pay for it. If you are selling something, you think it is worth this amount. If I am buying it, I think it is worth less. The only fair way is to sell it. You get what you get and then be done with it.

Property

If you have property and have to deal with family members, have it appraised because they feel it is worth a certain amount (usually a lot more than its true value). Get three appraisals and take the middle ground.

If it is a business and they have it evaluated themselves, they're going to pick the highest number. The solution is to let them put it on the market and try to sell it. This will show them what it is really worth.

Different types of businesses have different value points. Some allow significant money for its name or brand while others, such as construction, don't.

I have bought and sold electrical businesses twelve times.

Figuring Your Net Worth

A general contractor customer of mine, Bob Edwards, taught me to figure my net worth at the same time every year. That way, you can see if you made any money that year. If it went up, you made money. If it went down, you didn't. I don't do the quarterly reports and things like that. All that matters is what you take home—what you have in your pocket.

I had an old partner who was not happy with what the employees were making. He thought they were making too much money. I told him, "If you're happy with what you're making, that's all that matters." That is your bottom line.

See What's Happening With Money In, Money Out

Every Sunday morning, I go through all of the bills for the week and see what departments they go to—employee pay, trucks, insurance, etc. They are added up every week, and I get a spreadsheet that shows where we are with money coming in and going out. If something is going sideways, I know it. Then, I get on the phone and speak to the project managers, and I ask, "Hey, what's going on?" As long as they're in the plus, I don't care what they're doing.

Protect Everything When You're Not Around

When I was in my 20s, I saw first hand what can happen to a company when this is not done. The owner passed away, and the wife took over the company. She didn't know what she was doing. The contractors were just driving around, not working. The company went south in less than 24 months.

I told myself, if she had closed the doors right then, she would have lived very comfortably for the rest of her life. Most people don't understand how overhead and expenses can get away from you. The silent killer is overhead in a business. It will kill you.

Here is what I have put in place...

If something happens to me, and I am no longer around, I have a safe deposit box that holds a letter of detailed instructions of what to do when I am gone and not to deviate from it. My wife and sons know about it.

It tells what to do, step by step, and who to call.

Spend It

Overhead: The Silent Killer

Overhead: people don't understand it, they don't get it. I think it takes about a year before you know what overhead is—if you are still around once you get done. The way to know if it is overhead versus just expenses—if you can bill it, it's not overhead. If you can't bill it, and you have to pay for it, it's overhead. If I can't bill someone for what I just did, it turns into overhead.

When my kids were in high school, we had some rental buildings. I gave them a pickup truck and a 200-gallon tank full of seal coat to cover the driveways and parking lots. They learned a lot about business, and it was hard work. It probably influenced them to stay in college.

We bought a self-serve car wash and had them run it so they could experience what it was like to run a business.

We deposited $1000 earned from the car wash into their business account, and they were so excited because they thought they had a lot of money. They were quick to find out that we owed for gas, electric, soap, water, and all the things that went along with keeping the business operating.

They said to me, after paying for all of that, "There's hardly anything left!" It was a rude awakening for my boys. It showed them at the early age of sixteen that it takes a lot to run one of these joints. We did that on purpose. Today, they still talk about it. That was 20 years ago.

To buy something for a dollar and sell it for three, the untrained eye might think there is a two-dollar profit. But in reality, to keep the doors open, the lights on and phones ringing, you actually lost money in that transaction. This is why so many business people struggle—not knowing enough about business but just enough to get themselves in a lot of trouble.

Reinvest

Too often, I see people who don't reinvest in their business.

We did a job for a rivet company that was owned and run by two brothers and a sister, second generation. I got a call from one of them to hook up a new machine. All the equipment they had was from their dad in the '50s. Each one had to have an operator because they broke down every day. We hooked up the new machine and watched it in action. It was like a finely tuned Swiss watch. When I told one of the owners that the machine was pretty cool, he replied, "Yes, it will replace ten machines. As long as we can keep feeding it material, it will run 24/7 and call us if it shuts down for any reason."

I asked him, "Then you can get rid of ten employees?"

He said, "Yes."

I then asked, "When are the other machines coming?"

He said that this one was expensive, and they weren't buying any more. Two years later, they were out of business. They couldn't keep up. They wouldn't reinvest. They had 50 old machines. If they reinvested in their company, they could have bought 5 machines, kept only 2 operators and got rid of the rest. If they sold 100 million rivets a year, and if they bought enough material to make the rivets, they could go ahead and keep the machines running to make 100 million. You wouldn't have to turn off the machine and change the dyes or whatever for something else. When you buy the raw materials, you are going to save a fortune. They wouldn't do that. They wouldn't replace an overabundance of employees with machines.

Between the old machines breaking down constantly, not enough material, and very high overhead for wages, they were unable to make a profit.

What People Don't See

This is what people don't see. You do a job and make $100,000, but you spend $110,000.

The biggest problem that contractors face is that they don't want to reinvest. Let's say you drop $150,000 on piping. Now, all of a sudden that pipe goes up 25-30%. You are never going to make 25-30% on your money in a bank. When pipe prices are up, and people are bidding, I can go in and undercut them because I paid 25-30% on my material.

Sign Your Own Checks

I am the only one who signs checks. When you are signing one, it is real money.

When I am out of town, there will be a rubber stamped check so they don't kick it back. The stamp is only good when I call the bank and let them know the checks are stamped.

Knocking Down Cost of Materials

There are many revenue streams in a business. Some are overlooked, and money is lost. In a business that uses materials in order to produce their final product, inventory becomes a key aspect.

When you buy materials and inventory them, you get a deeper discount as well as additional profits by buying materials at the times of the year when the prices are lowest. For us, it's 15% additional savings on material.

Taking into account how much it costs for labor to make your product and material, you can figure out how much you're gaining or losing in profits. For my company, it is 50% labor and 50% material.

Even though you would be saving 15% on material by buying in bulk and at the best time of the year, the true savings on the final product is 7.5% because you have to factor in the labor costs. 50% means you divide by two.

So, to put your money in the bank and make 1% or 2% versus stocking up material, we make an additional 7.5%. It could be more or less for other businesses. Either way, the more you use in material, the more significant it becomes to your bottom line.

For instance, $1,000,000 of material inventory will bring $150,000 in additional profit.

Labor is the Only Variable

When I bid a job, the costs are 50% material and 50% labor. We talked about how to save on material and improve the bottom line. The only variable that I have is with labor.

If I bid on a job, and it is going to require 1,000 hours, I can save 20% on the labor because I have already invested in the tools, trucks, and improved productivity every way possible to make the labor easier and faster. We have a bidding platform that we bid off of, and all of my competitors bid on it. So, if I can save 20 points at $100 an hour, we are looking at a $20,000 reduction in labor costs by investing in the tools.

Look at how you can improve productivity, especially if labor is your only variable, because you have to make sure everything (workflow, tools, heavy equipment, etc.) is in order so you can save more money on labor. Just like buying material at the right time of the year, improving labor often allows me to get more jobs by bidding lower than my competition. This is another way you can either improve your bottom line for higher profit or get more jobs because you'd have more room to outbid your competition.

Keep It

When Can a Startup Draw Money?

You don't draw from the company for seven years.

General "Cadillac" Contractors

Some people who go into business don't understand success because they can't distinguish cash flow, overhead and profit. They start to see money and think they are rich. It leads into what I call "Cadillac" contractors. This guy would take the 25-30% you made buying material wisely and spend it on himself. Instead of buying a tool that they need, they go and buy a Cadillac. That Cadillac doesn't make them money. I have a truck that has 125,000 miles on it, and the wheels are falling off. Nobody gave me a job because I had a nice truck. My motto is: I hope they buy good tools because I will buy them when they go out of business.

Here you have a Cadillac contractor. He goes and buys the biggest truck or car so everyone will think he's successful, and yet he hasn't paid the phone or electric bill. They see money that isn't theirs and have a false sense of success. He's got an ego. He's going to the country club, flashing money around, and his wife has gotten all the extra work on her body. He won't give that up even though he has gotten himself into hot water. Me, as a contractor, when I see that, I know he is going to pay himself first to retain that image. You are at the bottom of the list for getting paid. Be careful ... he is not going to give up the country club, so he is not going to pay you.

Example, an electrical contractor is hired to do a million-dollar project. The general contractor owes them half a million dollars, plus the electrical company already has a quarter of a million dollars in materials and labor into the project, making a debt of $750,000. The general gets a call from a lighting fixture vendor that the electrical company bought lights from and asks when the general will be releasing payment. They haven't been paid on the light fixtures, so the first thing they'll do is not pay me.

There is one construction contractor that does five to seven billion in sales a year. Take six billion, and divide it by 365 days. That is your average amount of money. Now multiply that by 60 days, and add four percent interest. That is what they are making by holding your money for

60 days. They cut you off, pay your suppliers, and you go bankrupt. They get someone else to finish the job for 200 grand.

Retiring

You have to know when to retire, when to pull the plug, when to get out. When that time is there, you will know. It is when you start to lose your drive. You are not waking up on fire like you use to. This isn't necessarily an overnight thing. You can gradually phase yourself off of the main lines by delegating more and relinquishing more of your responsibilities over time.

Pretend You're Broke

An old customer of mine by the name of Dave O'Mally used to say, "We all have an imaginary financial line." It's your comfort line. An unexpected bill comes up—your motor drops out of your car. It costs 5-6 thousand dollars. Now, you went below that line. So you are going to save, work harder, do what you have to do to get back up to that line. When you are at the comfort line, you become content and lax. Go above the line, and you will splurge.

Understanding this imaginary line, you can use it to great advantage. You can create an imaginary emergency. I wake up every morning and pretend that I'm broke. My cost of labor is so heavy that I have to be at the company or they will walk out the door. This is a very powerful thing that will keep you in overdrive.

You can also physically create this urgency.

Years ago, when my kids were young, we paid our house off with double and triple payments. Six months later, I asked my wife, "How are we doing? Are we saving any money?" With the significantly lower monthly expense, I thought she was going to tell me we had a nice nest egg growing.

She said, "No, we have all these bills with the kids and so forth."

So, I went to the bank and took out a mortgage. I put that money into an account and, even with the same paycheck amount, we were able to make the mortgage payment. I did that 3 times over. When you do that, you are tricking yourself that you are broke. I created the urgency to pay the mortgage. This resulted in finally being able to save money because these mortgage payments were untouchable. They couldn't be spent on the kids' bills and so on. It is very common to spend more as you make more. This is a clever way around that.

The Best Kind of Car to Drive is One That's Paid For

You can lease anything, but the best kind of vehicle is a paid one. Don't waste your money on a showy car. You just need to get your butt from point A to point B. A vehicle should be a utility. You can spend a lot less money impressing others with respectable clothing or even uniforms if your company is appropriate for it. IF someone wants to date you because you have a fancy car, you're asking for undue hardship because this kind of thing has no business in choosing relationships and likely will not work out in the long run.

Set Aside for Employees

Take your sales for the previous year and divide it by the number of employees that you have. That is going to tell you how much money you need to pay your electricians or whatever kind of production employees you have for your company. Production employees are the ones who make your products or deliver your services. Leave that money in your Cash Receivables accounts for your business so you have room to breathe. This is also insight into money you can see that is not yours, and you don't spend it like a Cadillac contractor.

When Extending Credit

In some businesses, credit is something you can't avoid because it's how the industry operates.

In our industry, I need to be a banker and an electrician. Our receivables are crazy. If we have done commercial work for a company and they don't pay, we can put a mechanic's lien on the property. After a lien has been created, we give a waiver saying we have been paid.

Here's how it works: we have ninety days from the last day we work on the job to put a lien on the project. We have to watch that, or we lose our rights to collect payment. If we give them a waiver before they pay us, and they wait to pay, I know they are holding onto the money to collect interest. The agreement is they pay in thirty, and if they're holding out for sixty or ninety days, that's when we drop the gloves and force the issue.

This is an extreme, and it doesn't happen a lot, but you

have to know about it. The lesson is, don't let people take advantage of you. Your attitude should be, *why should they be making the interest when I can be?*

A situation like this needs to be watched. I have to make sure I get paid within 90 days of the last day of work, or I lose it just like that. I start asking, "Why isn't this paid?" Find out what is going on. You have to use your brains and be willing to get in there to figure it out. Don't accept words. If the home owner has a big ego, you will need to have the guts to stand up to his subtle aggression.

He may be aggravated that you're bothering him with this frivolous matter even though he said he would pay. If he hasn't paid anything, if he isn't paying even smaller amounts, he is only giving you fast talk. You can't accept words for money, and you have to be diligent about it. They know, and you need to remind yourself, that 90 days goes by extremely fast. The closer you get to the end date, the more power the customer can feel s/he has over you.

You have to be careful because they can get into a challenge with you. It becomes about proving s/he has the upper hand more than ethically paying their debt to you.

You have to know the personalities of people so you know what you can expect from them.

When extending credit to a customer, be alert to their financial behavior. Do they have a huge ego and seek to impress? Are they driving a big, fancy car, living in a big house, member of a country club ... the whole nine yards? They are going to pay themselves before they pay you.

You better be careful if they fall behind on paying you.

Eventually, they are not going to pay because they have to keep their image up with their friends. It happens to us all the time. A lot of this pertains to us having to extend credit. If you keep an eye on such a person and put the pressure on at the first sign of faltering, you stand a better chance of collecting all or most of their debt before they go under. Putting pressure on this type of client is your best bet of getting your money.

Collect First, Fight Later

Annie and Lewis, owners of Annie Properties and the first developers of the West Loop in Chicago, taught me to first collect what you can, then fight. I had a colleague who told me this, and I was floored by its simplicity and common sense.

Three Months' Cash on Hand

I try to keep 3 months' cash in hand. I have my own personal line of credit and a lot of credit for the company. If you are going to try to fly by the seat of your pants without having the credit to back it, you are going to have a lot of problems. You have to have at least 3 months' worth of what it costs to operate.

Barriers To Spending

I tell people, "If you have money, put it in a spot where it's hard to get at because you'll be less likely to do something foolish with it. You won't make the impulsive buys."

I put all of my personal money in a place where it takes

me two days to get it. That eliminates impulse buying. The "I deserve" mindset will ruin you on the spending. These people come up with a boat, car, whatever, saying, "I deserve that."

George K's Ten Percent Rule

A friend of mine, one of my dad's partners, always used to say to me, "Kid, if it costs you 10% more to go first class, go first class in your life."

I will always remember that. If you can work 10% harder, you will be first class. Stay that extra hour to take care of someone, and you will be fine in your life. That is all it takes. Ten points to go first class; to do things in a better way, to donate, to be the best.

What George meant was, you are already doing what you are doing, and to simply add 10% more effort, efficiency, zest, passion ... you can do so much more. The difference is exponential.

6

BUSINESS FUNDAMENTALS

When Buying an Existing Business

When I bought my company, I didn't know it at the time, but I did something that ended up being pretty smart. I bought from someone who was ready to retire.

Don't go with the guy who's 40. Go with the one who wants to retire.

When people are at the point of relinquishing their authority, delegating more and slowing things down for themselves, they're going to share all of their knowledge with you; even the really amazing stuff they've learned. This is priceless because you can't buy this kind of knowledge. The best information is held closest to successful people's chests.

You also have an opportunity to get a better price. The existing owner, Bill, was just looking to keep a little money coming in, and that would be fine.

Palos Electric was upside down when I bought it. Bill was 70 and recently had a heart attack. His employees started taking advantage of him by slacking. Under the circumstances, I had gotten a good deal.

To this day, he is the smartest guy in the industry, hands down. He taught me how to bid accordingly and told me, "Let everyone outbid each other in the spring, and you'll get your margins in the fall."

Gullibility is a Vulnerability

Honest people think that no one else would ever be dishonest. People who play fair think that no one will cheat. The honest guy or girl believes no one will lie. Wrong expectations and gullibility are just two points of ignorance the budding entrepreneur often suffers. Usually with great financial loss if not total failure.

Honesty in Business

You have to be honest in business. If you lie, you have to have a great memory. Don't be tempted to cheat the system for an easier route. There is no easy route.

Don't be tempted to cheat or lie. You have to always think about the long game. It's never about a big fix right now but more about the marathon of constant steps in the right direction.

The person willing to cheat their way will always be looking over their shoulder. It may be frustrating when the dishonest guy drives by in his new car, but think of it this way—you stand no chance of being arrested or closed down for fraud. Don't make yourself a potential target. The honest person comes out of IRS investigations with flying colors. You can't say that much for the guy who cheats for personal profit.

I have a motto: if everyone tells you to bet on the Bears, go the other way because they are going to lose. People have a tendency to speak from a position of authority. In other words, everybody is an expert. If you were to listen to everyone you know, you would literally find yourself going in circles. This is where knowing who you are talking to becomes very valuable. How do you know? Look at their level of success. You can't just believe what they tell you about their achievements. If you can't look the guy up and find something like he was the CEO of a successful company or founder of this or that, don't take their advice.

You don't want everyone in your corner telling you that you're going to win.

Positivity has its place, but you need to have at least one or two individuals who will tell you like it is. Sometimes it's hard to see what's really going on when you're in the middle of things. When someone takes a look and sees that you are headed toward a cliff, they better damn well tell you so. Then you will realize it is a complete bust and chalk it up to a loss.

You have to lose the "I deserve" mindset when you are in business. In this day of entitlement and "I get to win too" attitude, you have to move away from that nonsense. "I deserve a better car. I deserve a better truck. I deserve more money..." You don't deserve anything. You only have the right to go and make it happen.

I don't care what business you're in; I see the same mistakes. All businesses have the same fundamentals, which you will read in this book.

My family and others I know listen to most of what I

have to say, and they learn from it. The majority of my knowledge was taught to me by others, and the rest was learned at a survival level.

Mistakes

I've made a lot of mistakes. When you are trying to succeed, you can't help but experience a lot of failure. Success is earned by people who learn from their mistakes. It is how you become wiser than your competition. After a while, you start to pull ahead because you're smart enough not to make those same mistakes again. Your competition blames the economy or other things for their shortcomings.

So, when you screw up, remind yourself that it is a rare opportunity to learn something invaluable. Figure out what you did or didn't do that produced this undesirable result. Try not to do it again, and hope to walk away wiser.

Make it Look Easy

If you make it look easy, you are doing a good job. If you make it look hard, you don't know what you are doing. It is never easy; it just looks easy. There is no luck involved; it's created.

Competition: Keep Your Mouth Shut

You can keep your mouth closed and keep them guessing, or you can open your mouth and take the guesswork out. Noticeable or not, your competition wants to know what you are doing. The most sacred information in your business is how you operate. Don't give out your trade secrets on a silver platter. That's just self-sabotage.

This also goes beyond trade secrets into areas like how well you are doing or how much business you had last month. Don't let anyone know your business, because guess what. They are going to move in down the street and go into direct competition with you. The more you talk, the more competition you'll have. Just keep your mouth shut and keep them guessing.

This applies to everyone in the company. I tell my employees that when they are talking to someone, pretend you are talking to a judge. In other words, keep your mouth shut.

Cadillac Mindset Will Hold You Back

One time, there was a person I was working with who drove up with a co-worker in his van. He mentioned he was going to buy a new van. I asked, "What's wrong with the one you're driving?"

He replied, "Nothing."

I was baffled and asked, "Then why are you getting rid of it?"

He said, "It's paid for, and the guy at the dealership said he'll give me a brand new one for the same monthly payment."

There was another time when a guy who received a settlement for a neck injury pulled up in a brand new Lincoln Continental. He wasn't working. He just came by to say hello. I asked him, "What're you doing with this car?"

He said, "It's from the settlement."

He didn't put the money in the bank or invest it in his future.

I've been a blue-collar guy my whole life. I just look at money differently. These are perfect examples of how people keep themselves at their comfort line. When they go below it, they scurry to get back up to it. But it's financial insanity. To incur long-term debt when you don't need to or blow sudden bursts of newfound income is being your own worst enemy.

Personal Story on Interest

The day after my graduation, I became an electrician. My dad gave me a brand new car for my high school graduation. In the glove compartment was the payment book. He said, "Here you go, kid. Here's the coupon book. Make the payments, and don't be late."

I paid the car off without missing a payment.

It is the only car payment I have ever had because when you take a loan, you pay a lot of interest, especially in the beginning. If you don't have to, don't. Most people who want you to think they have money don't. The best car that you can own is one that is paid for. Just remember that those big buildings aren't being paid for by guys like me. They're from all of the interest from all of the loans out there.

Do What You Have to Do

My mentors also taught me how to deal with uncomfortable situations. We can be reasonable about doing what we know we should do.

When I was having a tough time laying someone off because it was an uncomfortable situation, he told me, "Go home, look at your kids, and tell them in your mind that they can't have something because you don't have the balls to lay this guy off. You will run in there tomorrow and lay this guy off and probably escort him out the door."

Know Every Job

In running a business, you have to know all the jobs and how they are done so you can correct when things go sideways.

W-O-R-K

We hear a lot these days about finding a job you love, and you'll never work a day in your life. This has merit but gives WORK a bad name. The times have been distorted into some fanciful thing about being happy every day and that all of life is a musical. People take this as meaning their job should be easy, simple and fun. This is not what the real world is like. If you think you're going to sit and paint pretty pictures all day and be a millionaire, you're in for a rude awakening. The wherewithal for success is completely missing from the equation. If, on the other hand, you paint a little each day, and the rest of the day, for the next ten hours, you promote and collect money that is owed you and do a hundred other things required, you have a much better chance. It's not about taking the path of least resistance. It's the complete opposite, which brings the greatest return for your efforts.

Now more than ever, if someone is willing to put the time in and get their hands dirty—it doesn't have to be construction; it can be anything—they can make a lot of money.

If it were easy, everyone would be doing it. If you take the hardest job in your industry and do it well, you are going to make a fortune. You have to take the dirtiest jobs—the jobs that no one else wants to do.

Buy the right tools, the right equipment, and do whatever you can to get very good, and you will do very well. As far as loving what you do, the truth is, if you take what you do seriously and realize what value you bring to others, you too can experience the enjoyment of work. It is only the person who tries to avoid work and never realizes their purpose who calls work a "four-letter word."

Balls in Aisle 3

To go into business, you need to have a set of balls. They can't be in your wife's purse or missing in action. If you think you might be someone who lets others push you around, or you have some back off when it comes to standing your ground, go to the Man Store, to Aisle 3, on the top shelf, and grab a set.

You have to be tough. Between customers wanting to take advantage of you, employees wanting to take advantage of you … whatever the case may be, you have to have big balls to go into business for yourself. If you expect to see success, you've got to have some stones to be able to do and say whatever it takes. You put everything on the line. You get up every day and take risks.

I tell people, "I do not gamble, but I gamble every day when I get up." I invest a lot of time, energy, sweat and money every day, gambling that I will get it back and make a profit from it.

So many things can go wrong in business. There's always a lot of money involved that you can lose—oftentimes money that is not yours. You have lenders, credit for inventory, utility bills and other entities you are accepting services from. You have employees working with the belief that you will give them a paycheck that won't bounce when they cash it. If you can't take risks like these and more, you need to step up and change that attitude, or go work for someone else. If you take the risk, you have the opportunity to make the kind of money with a business of your own.

That's part of the drive that can create the strength needed for business. It's a matter of survival, a matter of how you choose to live your life and what you want.

Ask yourself whether you are willing to compromise your goals and dreams for playing it "safe". Or are you willing to risk everything for a better life for yourself and those who work with you?

People generally want to knock you down if you are successful. This is another reason you need a set of balls. You have to be tough, stand your ground on what you believe is right, and keep on going.

The answer is crystal clear. Either grow a set, or go to Aisle 3 and buy yourself a pair.

Ego Versus Self-Worth

Attitude, mindset, the way you think of yourself … affect your actions and performance. If you don't have the right opinion of yourself, you're going to crave it from others. You can also end up acting foolishly and be a detriment to your company and success.

If you have a big ego, you spend your time patting yourself on the back. It's a never-ending appetite for praise and validation. Ego comes from a place of insecurity while self-worth comes from a position of strength.

If someone seeks validation from others, they tend to do dumb things like brag about company trade secrets or how their industry is super lucrative. There goes their piece of the pie being divided up by the new competition!

Self-worth, on the other hand, is about experiencing achievement. It's how well or poorly you've done things and how you feel about yourself with regard to those outcomes. Basically, if your self-worth is low, you replace it with a big ego.

Self-worth is taking count of what you have achieved. The more successes you make, the greater the confidence and inner feeling of accomplishment you have. You've built your company from scratch or brought it back from ruin. You took many risks when most people wouldn't dare. You've gone through the sleepless nights wondering where your next paycheck is going to come from. Risk after risk, you dare to do what most people would crumble over. And inch by inch, you start to build a thriving business.

It should be clear by now that ego is no good and self-worth is utmost when it comes to success. Some people want to go around and tell others what they have earned and done. This is not good because it comes from a place of weakness. People with an ego also tend to belittle the people around them, thinking they are better than everybody else.

You need to build up your self-worth; it's something you have to have. But the only way to earn self-worth is to overcome the struggles, challenges and fears, and make something happen from nothing. Worry builds self-worth, whether it is wondering if you are going to be able to sell what you have to offer or get the job you need or be paid for what you've delivered. Self-worth and success go hand-in-hand. You really can't have one without the other.

What's interesting is, there are more people with egos than there are people who know their self-worth. The only way to become more self-assured, self-confident and realize your greatness is by doing a lot of daring things. Most people just don't have it in them to take such risks and constantly live on the edge. So when you see a guy bragging about this and that, you can be pretty sure he's as insecure as they come.

You can have an ego and award yourself for about 10 minutes. Just don't tear your rotator cuff by patting yourself on the back. It's time to get back to work.

Don't desire to have others think you're great. Don't feel it necessary to be thanked for a job well done. Why? Because most of the time, you're just not going to hear it. You may damn well deserve it, but it just doesn't come. And then you feel like a complete loser, starved for more validation. You don't get your self-worth from the compliments and thank you's of others.

If you have self-worth, you won't need validation from others. That's a really good thing.

I guess what I'm trying to say here is, remain humble, remember where you started from, and don't get a big head in thinking you are better than others. Confidence and self-worth keep you grounded and able to think right. If you base your decisions on a perspective of ego, you are no longer capable of seeing what is actually right in front of your nose. Like wearing rose-colored glasses, you see things in an altered state where you are invincible and others are disposable.

A confident person treats self and others with respect. Another dead giveaway that someone lacks confidence is when they try to position themselves much higher than everybody else. It's one thing to be the boss, it's another to talk down to people.

Struggle Forces Strength

There is oftentimes competition between siblings, and the younger ones are bent on proving that they can run faster and jump higher. When it comes to going into business with siblings, unless there is an unusual relationship, the younger one is going to try to prove he is smarter. This is an unhealthy relationship because it becomes more of a battle of wits than it is working together under a common goal. It is going to fail and bring down the business.

As I say elsewhere in this book, "From failure comes wisdom." But also, "From struggle comes strength and appreciation of overcoming impossible odds." Just like a child who is not allowed to struggle and figure things out, the life-changing values only available to those who risk everything are never realized.

One of the many things I learned from struggle was that nothing happens on its own. I think one of the most detrimental traits people are hindered by is to think that all of the success happens automatically.

My boys went into business for themselves. The hardest thing for a parent is not to help their kids financially. They needed to struggle, and now they are very successful. I made sure they had food on their table, but I didn't buy them cars or pay for any of that. They had to struggle, and I knew that was the best lesson for them. Most parents will give them everything, and that is usually when they fail.

When the boys started on their own, I made sure they both worked for people that I knew. When they were ready to leave, I told them to make sure that they leave as an ally. If you leave the wrong way, they will be your enemy. Today, they appreciate where they are, not taking anything for granted.

You can't buy self-gratification; you have to earn it. That is why I didn't want my sons to take over my business. There would have been no self-gratification.

I learn something every day. Be willing to learn. In business, you can't take your foot off the gas. When things are going well, don't coast. They don't stay the same.

I have customers who want me to think they have a ton of money. They have huge egos and have the need to make others think they are successful, but they are not making a lot of money. This kind of customer is dangerous.

Guess who is at the bottom of the priority list on getting paid? That's right—you! S/he is busy blowing their cash on image instead of their obligations.

When I see this kind of big shot, flashy guy strutting around, jetting off here and there, I watch the Receivables. If I see this customer's debt with us creeping up, then I bypass the admin person and personally jump in and start putting the pressure on.

Now, you can be tripped up by evaluating the wrong things. For instance, the car they drive or the clothes they wear are not what you look for. Anyone can put on a good act with a leased car and a thousand-dollar pair of shoes.

You can see it coming. Don't let them get in deep with you. If you are dealing with a customer with a huge ego, you are probably going to get hurt more often than with a customer who doesn't have an ego.

If someone says, "I will never work for them again because they didn't pay me," they are doing me a favor. I don't want to work for them either.

Stand up For Your Employees

If you're too cocky with people, you're not going to make it. People won't want to work with you, and you'll get a bad reputation.

In the beginning of your career, you may have to put up with a lot of BS from people. It would be good business sense to choose your battles wisely and, for the most part, lose them all in the beginning of your career in order to win the war long term. You can't let your own pride get in the way of your survival and success.

Just the same, you will reach a point in your career where you can be more particular about who you choose to deal with. In other words, you have some leeway for telling one or two customers to take a hike. The more successful you become—and this is one of many incentives for becoming a big success—the more you can keep your integrity intact. In your early days, you may find yourself graciously making a lot of wrong customers right, all with the best smile you can muster. There will come a day where you won't have to put up with the few jerks who honestly don't deserve your great products and services. Or they at least deserve to be put in their place, and you're just the guy or gal to do it.

It also becomes a point of respect from your employees. You can't let someone belittle you or them.

We were all having lunch one day when the general contractor from the job we were on came up, beating his chest, and said, "Well, so far, you guys are doing okay. We'll see about using you in the future."

This is just an abuse of a position of power. This guy wanted us to quiver in our seats and beg for some bread and water so we could live to see another day. All due to his grace and kindness to us lowly peons.

The truth was, this guy was nothing without us. We were

the ones who would make him look good or look like a fool to the customer.

I looked at the electricians. I could see them all smirking because they knew what was coming. I said to him, "You know, I kind of put you to the test too. You haven't paid me a thing yet. Not only were you testing me, and you already told me I passed, I think you should know you're failing miserably."

The guys all start laughing while the surprised GC tried to wipe the embarrassment off his face. He knew we were the best. That's why we were hired.

What kind of bull is that—trying to embarrass me in front of my electricians?

This is an example of not having to take the unjustified abuse from others. Be willing to walk away from a job because it's not your only one.

He walked away not knowing what the hell to do. One thing for sure he wasn't going to do was try that again. He showed more respect moving forward.

You still have to be careful. You have to be smart. Let the other guy shoot his mouth off first and make the wrong move, then you can blast him.

Be and Do What Counts

You can spend your days trying to please everybody and trying to get everybody to like you, but that's an impossible goal. Be what is more important to people, and you'll do just fine.

I tell my vendors I'm the biggest asshole they'll meet ...
but I'm the best-paying asshole. And you know what?
They wish they had more assholes for customers.

If you do what you promise, you'll have everything you
need. When materials are scarce, guess who's going to get
the bulk of their inventory. You, because they know you're
going to pay them, and on time.

It's nice to be liked, but it means nothing in life and
business. So if you feel like you have to walk on egg shells
around people because you might upset them, your efforts
can be better spent on keeping your word and fulfilling
promises.

There is a big difference between being liked and being
respected and trusted. When the chips are down, who
do you think people are going to come to, the nice guy
everybody speaks well of, or the person who never lets
people down and gets the job done on time as promised?

The real worth in someone is counted by what they DO.
That trumps everything else like saying nice things or
being a sweetheart of a guy or gal.

This is not to say you have to be a real SOB. The fact
remains that you cannot be both types of people and succeed. You're going to need to be a prick when the situation
calls for it and considerate when the time is right.

Be the person people can trust, and you will be a very
valuable person to others.

The Art of Communicating

There is an art to talking. There's too much texting and emailing today when it should be in-person communication. Face to face, I can tell if you're angry. I can tell if you're excited. I can tell if someone is giving me a load of bull. I can tell by body language. You can't do that when you're texting. It is important to go talk to people.

So many guys who taught me business sense were the handshake generation. Those days are gone. Now it is all about texting and emailing. They do it for security because it puts things in writing. A person's word is not what it used to be. I hate to say it, but in today's environment, it is necessary to get things in writing. I recommend you talk face to face and then document what was said with an email.

Don't Needlessly Create Competition

I am a stealth contractor. I don't like to be seen, and I don't socialize. It's just who I am. I lie in the weeds. Oddly enough, this has been to my advantage.

There was a company that, when they first started, had ratty trucks with bald tires, rusting out bodies ... They were in a field with little to no competition. When the owner started making money, he bought fancy trucks, all chromed out and showy. Well guess what? He has a lot of competitors now.

When others see you with the nice trucks, they want to be rich like you, so they decide to do what you are doing. You just created your own competition.

We don't patent tools anymore. We did in the past, but people copied and mass-produced them. We had just given our competitors an edge. Now, when we develop something, we have it made and don't tell anyone. We don't show anyone. Most people can't think for themselves and are always on the lookout to copy what others do.

When Working for Friends and Family

I get a lot of customers who want me to do something at their house or their mother's or father's house. Whatever the case may be, I can't bill them. They don't understand the wages. So what I do is tell them to make a donation to a charity. I recommend a charity. I get more miles out of that than charging them. They remember they donated to a charity.

Open Your Mail

Opening the mail as the owner applies to small companies. It might not work for large companies.

If you want to know what is going on with your business, open your mail. Your whole system comes through the mail, not just past due invoices or bank statements. It's like taking the pulse of your company.

In our electrical business, you can tell if someone is ordering materials not related to their job. That opens the door to theft and abuses with being overcharged. Someone else opening the mail doesn't check that. It's your money, and no one will treat it like you. They will never go the extra mile to save that extra point or check to see if something was overcharged.

Don't have someone else open it. You are going to know if you are behind on something or if something is not right. I am the only one who opens mail in my company. If I am on vacation, it sits in a bag on my desk.

Also, if a company calls and wants more work done but hasn't paid their bill, you have to tell them, "You pay your bill, and we'll send the people for the new job." This is why you open the mail; you know where everything is at.

The Four Experts You Need on Your Team ... The Super-Trifecta

You need a knowledgeable accountant, a good attorney, the right banker, and a great doctor. You need all four of them, and you better get the best there are. If you're missing one of them, you're eventually going to have a problem.

When it comes to accounting, I believe a lot of people make a mistake in hiring bargain accountants. I have heard so many business owners complain about what their accountant charged them.

I say, "Look, if your accountant knows what he's doing and saves you money, why do you care what he charges?" Where the problem lies with most people is they look at what someone else makes, not what they are getting for their investment. That causes a problem down the line. One looks for a cheaper accountant who is not that good, and the next thing you know, you're in trouble with the IRS or whatever the case may be. It's not worth it. Hire the best. Of course they cost more, but it's worth it.

As for legal matters, be wary of the attorney who tells you it is always about winning. Sometimes it isn't about winning. A person or company may have done something that was wrong, and you have every right to take them to court. It's better to walk away than to spend the time and money to get satisfaction of being told you were right. Choose your battles wisely, and realize that others often gain even when you lose. Their thought process will be very different from yours.

Then if you get an ambulance-chasing attorney, the next thing you know, you are upside down with the lawyer.

You need to have a banker who will work for you. If you need something, they can do it fast. You need to have a small bank that has the lending power for your needs. Make sure you deal with the head of the bank, not the person who doesn't have the authority to make decisions. In a small bank, the president or CEO is accessible.

You need to have a line of credit for your business. The bank will want to see your personal tax returns, the corporate tax returns, the year-end statement, and your personal financial statement. They compare year to year, not what you are doing presently. The bank will usually know when you are in trouble before you do. Without that, you can get yourself in deep.

As an example: the bank was renewing my line of credit. They asked why my labor spiked and materials were down. I didn't know why and had to look into it. They caught that and I didn't. It could be an inside problem.

And with the doctor, it is self-explanatory. You don't want to end up the richest guy in the cemetery.

Stick With What You Know

When my boys started their insurance business together, I gave them a big toolbox with nothing but a phone book in it. I said, "Listen, boys, stick with the insurance. If you need something done, call them. Don't mess it up yourselves. Stick with what you know."

The mentality of many business owners is to "do it yourself to save money," but this too often works out to be more costly and can even be dangerous.

7

FINANCE

MONEY, It's Not Just a Number

When I was still wet behind the ears as a businessman, one of my mentors Joe Basic taught me a great lesson about the value of money. This very smart man asked me, "If there were a hundred dollar bill on the floor, would you arm wrestle me for it?"

I told him, "I'd beat you over the head for it."

He said, "Good ... remember that. When someone owes you a hundred bucks, make sure you go and collect it."

Don't think a hundred is not a lot of money.

If someone owes you a hundred bucks, it's a hundred bucks owed you. Make sure they pay what they owe you.

To not collect is to allow them to be in debt with you. That can be more cruel than chasing them up and collecting. Why? Because you allowed someone to live with the guilt and burden of being in debt.

One time, there was a secretary of a customer of ours who had made the comment, "It's only 100 grand that they owe."

I stopped and asked her, "Would you let someone who owed you a thousand dollars not have to pay you?"

She said, "No way! I'd get my money."

I then said, "So, how does 'only' fit in the same sentence as 100 grand?"

She got my point.

Whenever I hear someone say, "It's only money," I get away from them because they don't respect what it represents. It's a dangerous path to take, especially when dealing with large amounts of money. Even $10, to treat it as unimportant is to invalidate what you have made with hard-earned sweat and guts.

8
Partnerships

Some partnerships are bad, others are worse. Partnerships almost never turn out well. You often have to deal with big egos and bad deals. Avoid them at all costs.

Don't get involved in a partnership that you don't know anything about. Don't get involved with someone who is looking at cheating.

You really have to scrutinize all opportunities that come your way. What are they bringing to the table? If you are bringing in money, what are they bringing in?

So many people try to have no-risk deals; they want to play with your money. You don't want to get involved in that. Whenever things go bad, they leave because they have no skin in the game. They have nothing to lose but their pride.

When you get into a business where decisions have to be made, that is where partnerships go sideways. With hindsight being 20/20, anyone can come in and be a critic. It can be very challenging to deal with partners, especially when they have big egos.

"Why did you do that?" … "Why didn't you do that?" …

That type of thing. I have never had any of them work. You need to have thick skin and the patience of a saint when dealing with partners. I've got the first one in spades, but I have little tolerance for critical people who think they could have done things better when they weren't even there when the ship momentarily sprung a leak and was going down fast.

I have only seen a few partnerships turn out well. So you have to be really careful. If you jump into an agreement with someone, you better know what you are doing. I think a lot of the problem is not enough communication.

I got involved in a partnership with a brick and mortar that went south. I was only a 20% partner, and when I signed the note, I signed stating it was for the 20%—thank God. When it came down to it, the bank wouldn't let me pay my 20%. If you get in as a minority partner, you better sign as only a minority partner for the loan and anything you sign. Otherwise, you are going to get yourself in deep.

I was very lucky that I didn't sign for 100%, or I would be on the books for owning a ton of money. The bank froze my son's special needs account, but when it was all done, I didn't pay the bank. They paid me because of what they had done to me. This is an example of why you better have a good attorney in the "Superfecta" section.

Stay Away From One-Sided Deals

My mentor Dave O'Mally introduced this scenario to me:

Someone comes to you and says, "Hey, I want you to be a partner in this retail shop."

You ask, "Okay, how is this going to work?"

"Well, you're going to put up all the money, and I'm going to run it."

When that is said, you should stop everything and walk away. Don't get involved, because when he gets tired of working at the shop, he goes home.

People behave very differently when they are working with another's money, not their own. When someone comes to the door with money in her hand as your partner is getting ready to close up, he will flip the OPEN sign to CLOSED right in her face and shut the lights without a thought about the sale he could have just made. He just made a customer feel unimportant. She'll go down the street to your competition and give them the money. It's only a matter of time before your non-invested partner drives enough people away. He's got nothing to lose. Meanwhile, you're out of all of the money.

You're now trying to manage the store along with your other business, and you can't.

If someone approaches me and wants me to be a partner, yet they are not putting any money in, I have nothing to do with them. If they are willing to put in the same amount I am, I will stick around to hear more. You want equal partnerships. Both need to pony up the same amount of money. Otherwise, I'm not going to bother. I recommend you do the same.

Never Invest in Pipe Dreams

Whenever people approach me to be a partner, and all they focus on is how much money we're going to make because of how much potential there is, they don't know what they're doing. They only have an idea—a pipe dream. There's nothing concrete to back up their claims. They don't have any concept of real costs, overhead, expenses and promotion for making something happen.

Anyone can dream up projected earnings based on the market size and other glamorous numbers. "If we were to only get 5% of this trillion-dollar market, we would be swimming in money."

Yeah, right. And I'm Mary Poppins and can fly in my dreams.

They have a shallow perspective. They are only looking at the end result; not how we're going to get way over to the other side of the great divide from where we stand today. There is nothing of value in their colorful words. Stay away from these dream chasers. They will only pull you off your course to wealth and happiness.

If someone wants me to invest in something and tells me, "Here is our exposure (risks/vulnerabilities for failure); here is what we stand to lose if things go south," I will listen to them.

The person has to be able to tell you the downside as well as the upside. The ratio should be something like: 80% downside data and 20% upside potential. The potential should be less important to you than the exposure.

The only way you know someone has done their homework and knows what they're doing is when they have considered worst-case scenarios and the risks involved. Whenever I get involved in a partnership, I want to know, "What is it going to cost me if things don't work out as planned?"

Real Estate Partnerships

The best type of partnership I've had that worked well was with real estate. It is cut and dried. You have rental units, you rent your spaces for X amount, pay the bills, and the amount that's left over is profit.

Most of my partnerships have been in real estate. I have had 4-5 partnerships in start-up businesses where I got a percentage of profits until paid off. Those worked out because I didn't run the business, and I had their houses as collateral (a lien on their house until the investment is paid off).

The only partnerships that seem to make it are the ones that do not get into each other's business. Someone approaches me about a partnership, I always figure the worst. What is my exposure (vulnerability to risk)? What will it cost me if it goes bad? Most people don't consider the potential downsides. If a guy comes in and only tells me how much we're going to make, I don't want anything to do with him. I want to know what it is going to take to make it and what our exposure is.

On Investment Partnerships

Example: let's say that Julie wants to go into business for herself, and she needs $100,000 to get things started. She convinces you to invest the money by signing over the $75,000 of equity she has on her house to you. The first thing you do is record it (put it on public record). You are not putting a lien on her house in this case because you are first in line for getting the $75,000 equity if things go south. This is a healthy partnership because you are taking a risk of $25,000, and Julie is risking the possibility of losing her house. You have to protect yourself.

As mentioned earlier, if you were to put up the $100,000 without serious risk for the other person, they would simply shrug their shoulders and say, "Oh well, we tried," and walk away.

Don't be the only risk taker. Ideally, you make sure that your partner is taking the greater risk or at least equal risk. Never be wooed over high interest or potential success. Most people will try to convince you that they are the good guy for letting you in on their million-dollar idea. Don't be a sucker. A lot of people operate on the rule, "Never use your own money." It's a terrible rule for everybody but the criminal who applies it to their business ventures. Don't ever work with someone like that. Such individuals are only willing to lose other people's money.

You Don't Want Ownership in a Company

You don't want ownership, or you will be on the hook for liability.

No Managing Partners

Also, there cannot be a managing partner because they can approve and sign all kinds of documents. The next thing you know, you have someone knocking on your door saying you owe them money. You say, "I didn't sign that," but it doesn't matter. You need to be careful with partnerships.

Don't ever sign over interest as a managing partner. The managing partner has full control over the partnership. If they want to borrow money, they can borrow money. If they want to sign off on a mortgage, they can do so. The other signature is not needed. The managing partner has the power to sign things without your signature.

If you have a bigger percentage than the other guy, he will try to undermine you. My partnerships are all the same. We all have equal rights; no one has the upper hand.

Every partner has different things they bring to the table. You can look at a partner and know if you are going to fit together. If they come in wearing a 3-piece suit and you're in your overalls, well, you know this isn't going to work.

Drugs, Alcohol and Gambling

If you are going to partner with someone, and there are drugs, gambling, or alcohol involved, you need to be very careful because that person is not going to be an asset but a liability. If it hasn't happened yet, it's just a matter of time. People cannot remain stable when they are involved with these kinds of volatile activities. Those are things to look at when you are picking a partner.

They start blaming you for their mistakes. You can take a calendar and be certain that there will be a date in the not so distant future where the company or partnership will end.

I have had a lot of partnerships. Once those things start happening, it starts going south. It's a cancer. It's either stage one or stage four, but it's going to take its course.

Never Drink with Your Boss

Don't ever drink with your boss. The potential for saying something you might regret is too great. They don't forget what you said, and it won't work out well.

9

EMPLOYEES

Employees need to have respect and trust for their employers. All my electricians have 100% faith in what I do, and I do everything in my power to keep them working. Without them, I am not here.

You won't hear me say, "He works for me." You will hear me say, "We work together." I do a lot for my employees. I put them on the highest pedestal. I will go to war for them.

The number-one thing with which to make people loyal to you is money and knowing that you would defend them if something were to go wrong in their lives. Stand behind them when it counts.

I pay my employees well, and I also run them hard, but you have to let them come up for air every now and then. I cut them loose once in a while when they have something important to do. I am a firm believer if something is important to one of my employees, it is important to me. And when it is personal—something difficult they're going through, for instance a divorce or a death in the family—I cut him some slack, a little bit of leeway. You've got to do that. I'm not saying get into their personal lives. The employees know that if something happens to them,

I will take care of them and their family. I am doing it because it is the right thing to do.

I tell them to go ahead and leave early but clock in for 8 hours. That is huge for them. I earn their respect by demanding high quality, and I gain their admiration by respecting their lives outside of work when it counts. If someone is in trouble, you help them. If you follow that in your business, you are going to be successful as far as employees are concerned.

Don't Flaunt It

I see too many business owners belittle their staff. There seems to be some misunderstanding of good leadership, and they think they have to position themselves as more superior.

I had an airplane years ago, and I lost a very good friend because of it. Though he was wrong, he thought that I could afford the plane because of how hard *he* worked. He thought it was unfair because it was his hard work that made it possible for me to afford a plane.

This showed me how employees think. Even if they are paid very well for their production, they feel unappreciated if you have more than them. Right or wrong, this is a fact of business.

The solution? If you have good employees you don't want to lose, then you should never drive a car that your employees can't afford, and don't live in a house they can't afford.

It is never a good idea to put yourself above your employees. Showing up to work in a $90,000 Mercedes, even when your employees are paid well, causes a rift and a feeling of imbalance and jealously. This is not a negative comment on employees; it is simple human nature, and even though you could be paying your employees well above the norm, it causes a sense of inequality. Drive the same trucks your employees drive. Have your wife drive the same car their wives drive. If you decide to splurge and go on a fancy vacation, don't post any photos on social media. The more you remain equal with your employees, the more camaraderie there will be.

Don't Tolerate Anyone Being Late

Probably the biggest downfall of a business is people being late. If you are late for a job, it costs money because there are three or four other guys who can't do their jobs because you're not there. Now the job isn't done today, and we have to go back tomorrow. It costs a fortune in my industry. This kind of thing slows down the schedule and draws out the completion date. In a lot of companies, big penalties can be given if deadlines aren't met.

When I hire someone, I tell them there are two things that will get you fired: 1) being late and 2) being late.

You can be the dumbest SOB in the world. We'll train you. But there are no excuses for being late.

How to Lower Your Employee Turnover Rate

I don't have the turnover of employees because I pay them well. I am probably 100% above the industry on paying my employees. They work their butts off, but they are paid well. Electricians don't leave me because 90% of them are paid foreman wages. That is the mistake the competition makes; they don't pay their people well, so their employees leave over the smallest upsets or better money somewhere else.

It's just good business to pay your employees well. If you don't, one could go to another company that pays better and tell them how you are doing things. Pay people well enough that they wouldn't even think of going somewhere else.

If employees are paid well, they are not going to leave you. They could make great money on their own, but their risk would be so great, they are not going to do it. They would have the worries and headaches I have with the financial side.

I would be struggling in business if I didn't pay my employees well. High turnover is deadly for any business. You end up paying more having to train new people and enduring the slow production period they go through than to simply pay your people well. There's more loyalty and productivity when it is at its highest level.

Project Managers Wear Three Hats

I have project managers/department heads who make a lot of money, but I don't have to babysit them. Their pay is predicated on what they make for the company. It eliminates them accepting jobs with bad paying customers.

My guys don't get paid until I get paid. They know this. They get a salary and a percentage of the profit. I don't have someone solely to collect money. It cuts down on overhead. They carry the responsibilities of Sales, Estimator and Collections all in one. They have to collect the money; I don't have to. So they are driven to collect. They have the relationship with the customer; I don't.

The project manager gets the work, collects the money and buys the material.

If you try to short someone on pay, they leave. You don't want a change of personnel in management or your customers will leave with that person because they have the relationship established with them. In my business, managers/department heads are paid union wages, which is a lot. Percentages are based on what they bring to the table. You have to be smart about it, and once you decide what percentage, you have to stick to it or they will be gone. Some companies decide to lower the percentage when money starts to get substantial, but it never works out. You can't reduce someone's pay once you've established it.

Don't worry about how much they are making. The whole objective is to keep the employees there, making money. Be happy with what you are making, and hopefully they make a billion dollars because that means you're making money too. You have to get someone who can do many jobs so you can pay that person more instead of having to get 3 people, which would cost a lot more, and each one would get less money and potentially be unhappy.

The percentage is set when they are hired. These guys know that I look at the books every week, and they will get phone calls from me if something doesn't look right. For instance, if sales are down, if they get a project and we're short on materials, or they haven't collected on a delinquent account, I'll ask why that is. It's important for everyone to know that the owner knows what is going on at all times.

This keeps people at their best.

How Much Should They Know?

People have a tendency to value what they should be paid for their work on the high side—the very high side. For some reason—even though they never have sleepless nights worrying how payroll will be met or the bills will get paid, where the next customer is going to come from, getting sued for something that happens at work, having to pay for the roof when it leaks or get up at 3 o'clock in the morning to check why the alarm went off, ad nauseam—they think their pay should be equal to the owner's. They're not bad people; it's just the way it is.

Ignorance makes people think and do illogical things. Just for the record, ignorance is not being dumb or much to do with IQ. It is when we don't know enough about something. It is a lack of knowledge or information about something in particular.

The people most likely to know your business are your office help—your admins.

Your first line of defense is to pay them well. They know more than most employees. Some usually know how much you make, how much money is running in and out of the company, and your dirty laundry.

You have somebody who balances your checkbook. They know what you make. This should be treated like the Coca-Cola® recipe: don't let any single person know everything there is to know. I have multiple checkbooks—some my personnel don't see—and that is where my pay comes out of.

What can happen if you don't do this? When it comes to raise time, that person now thinks s/he should be earning what you make. That is usually when you have a problem. Anything can come of this, such as embezzling money, because they think they're getting the short end of the stick. Even though they're dead wrong, it happens more often than you might imagine.

This is by no means foolproof to the vindictive person, but doing all you can to defuse these kinds of things is just smart business.

This might sound like a bad idea, but if you think about how costly it is to have to hire and train a new employee, you're saving money by keeping your employees and paying them well.

If someone hasn't said it already, I'll be the first to say, "Action is a best practice of any business." Do all you can by treating your good employees well. What do you do with the bad ones? You shouldn't have any. If you do, it means you're leaving the company vulnerable for something bad to happen one way or another. Action would apply here as well. If you leave a destructive person lurking around, it's only a matter of time before something happens that could have been avoided.

Poison in the Ranks

Remove any cancer in your company, no matter how good they are. Everyone else will pick up the slack.

I had the best electrician ever, but he had a mean streak and demeaning personality. Everything he said and did had a negative darkness to it. He was basically poison. When I got rid of him, they all picked up the slack, and it was like a burden was lifted. They said, "I'm glad you got rid of him. I wanted to quit."

When you have someone who brings the whole group down, it outweighs any abilities they have. It causes more harm than good for the company. It is going to hurt you in the short term but benefit you in the long run.

Christmas Bonuses

If you think the last point was uncommon, wait till you hear this....

We don't do Christmas bonuses. Let me explain, then you can judge me.

The reason is because if you do it once, it will be expected every year. The "bonus" part of it is completely ignored.

If not from the employee, then it comes from the spouse because they also expect it.

"I/You worked just as hard as last year and deserve the bonus!"

Let's say your company has a bad year, and you don't have extra money for the bonus, but they already bought a new washer and dryer on Black Friday with the money they expected to get from the bonus. It causes a rift. They turn into accountants instead of electricians. They start worrying about that instead of getting the job done.

In National Lampoon's *Christmas Vacation* movie, "Sparky" Griswald ordered a pool with the bonus he was expecting to get. Of course, Hollywood makes the business owner out to be a greedy ogre as they always do, but in the real world, there are up and down years. Don't jeopardize the relationship with your employees with this volatile activity. Pay them well, treat them right, and avoid this dilemma by never getting caught into this no-win situation.

10

THE CARDS ARE STACKED AGAINST YOU

Is it okay that people get paid more money being unemployed than they do when they have a job? Do you think it's okay that people who choose not to work don't have to pay taxes? And the people who work have more than 30 percent of their earnings taken from them and given to the guy who won't work? Does anybody *really* believe they should get a trophy just for participating? Should you get to play in the game even though you don't show up for practice?

I'm not making this up. Such laws are being passed. The Illinois school system has a mandate that forces coaches to give every kid on the team equal play time, even if they don't show up for practice.

This is just the continuation of the propaganda from people who were indoctrinated before you. They've been told everybody is entitled to the things others have even though they haven't lifted a finger. They've been taught to hate anyone who is successful and that the rich deserve to have their money taken away from them and spread out among the crowd whether they are workers who contribute something valuable to society or who only take from society.

This even starts with childhood. Take the children's tale about the fictional "hero" Robin Hood, for example. Anyone with money is described as greedy and loathing to all people. The heroes and favorable humans are the meek and poor. And they have a right to steal from those despicable rich people.

So, to even think about becoming successful can bring up personal conflict of "being a bad person" or the indoctrinated hatred and jealousy that comes from the crowd. They've been trained to hate anyone who doesn't agree with them, and they attack without reservation.

Things work in a village, city, state, or country when everybody contributes in some way. The few who are unable to because of age or physical impairment should be taken care of, but the real number is about three percent of a population, not 35 percent.

Like I said, this isn't about me, and though it might sound like it, this is not political either. It's just impossible to not at least bring up politics, bureaucracy and indoctrination, if only to shed some light on where much of the BS is coming from. More than that is to just make you aware that the cards are stacked against you being successful.

Now, this shouldn't make you give up. It should get you pretty pissed off. It should light a fire under you that makes you even more determined.

11
WHY DOES SUCCESS SEEM SO HARD?

Many of us entrepreneurs do okay, but we don't hit our highest goals. In order to start winning in a way that's worth writing home about, you need to become aware of a few influences that are tipping the scales away from your favor.

There are a lot of flaws in the world created by people who, for whatever reason, never seem to stop and think about the long-term effects of their actions. You would think I am referring to others, but we all do it to some degree. And although some people have made it their life's mission to go around messing things up, what's important is what we can learn from our own mistakes and the screw-ups of others.

It always seems like the rest of us have to spend time cleaning the dung off of our shoes from the BS of the best laid plans of others. Yet they never seem to suffer such consequences.

But you know what? It doesn't matter. What matters is what you do, and when you mess up, you fix it.

Why Failure is Common

There's something about commonality, popularity and being part of something that makes people do the grandest things; no matter how bizarre or destructive. Plus, there's a push from the current doers to convince more people to join in. Some profit from it, like drug dealers. Others just feel better about themselves because they're not the only ones doing it.

It is difficult not to be influenced by what everybody else is doing, and you now tend to copy their behavior, no matter how dumb it might be. No matter how demented or idiotic, it seems to be the way to do things. Like an unspoken agreement, it just seems okay when everyone around you is doing it.

Interestingly, that's the furthest thing from the truth. If you're doing what everybody else is doing, the way they're doing it, you're screwed. You might as well pack everything up and get in line at the nearest food kitchen. At least that way you'll save yourself decades of frustration and misery trying to be successful and finding your personal bliss. You never will. Personal bliss? Are you kidding me? Who thinks this stuff up anyway? Maybe somebody who needed to sell more tee shirts.

Winning the lottery wouldn't even solve things because you'd be broke soon enough, even with millions of dollars. Just look at the majority of lottery winners. This isn't my opinion. It's simple fact backed by historical data and observation.

This might really be terrible in a lot of ways, but there is a silver lining if you believe, understand, and take action with this one thing. For whatever reason, it seems the masses do destructive things way more than constructive.

This means that if you can keep yourself mostly free of the foolish things people do and learn to do what successful, happy people do, you're going to be more successful in life than you ever thought possible. This falls into who we should be rubbing elbows with.

In all honesty, I'm not completely certain that it's the majority that's being destructive. I say this because it could simply be good marketing campaigns and propaganda that lead us to believe "everybody's doing it."

The point is, whatever "everybody" is doing, you need to strongly consider the potential drawbacks. In other words, take a good look for the booby traps and pitfalls because they're almost certain to be there.

If you have the slightest doubt about this, your next step should be to put this book down and take a walk or ride around your town for a bit. It won't take long to see the destructive things people do, like they're normal and okay.

As an example that may or may not be exaggerated, if one person or just a few people were to start doing something idiotic like cutting their right ear off, they'd be put away—ostracized from society. But if enough people started doing it, it would likely catch on. More and more people would do it, and cutting your right ear off would become acceptable behavior. Not the *left* one … heaven forbid if you were to cut the wrong ear off!

Let's stick with what's happening now and be a little more

realistic. What becomes acceptable by the masses is truly astonishing.

I'm not perfect by any means. I'm not here to tell you of the dumb things I do, and, as most would probably agree, there are plenty. What I say next is to make a point and not judge.

We see people excessively drinking. We see them gambling away their paychecks or taking drugs or any number of destructive things. We're clever at making things look civil and respectful. Hiding champagne in a tall, classy glass of orange juice doesn't *really* hide the fact that you're drinking alcohol in the morning. But look at how many people do this at least every Sunday morning. Oh, and that's to "help" with their hangover from the binger the two previous nights! I'm just saying ... look at the crazy things we do.

Look, I'm no prude. I'm not trying to say we can't have some fun now and then or do things in moderation. My point is that people in the main go too far with things.

Look at the crap most people eat, in excess no less. Then take a look at how drastically the health of the United States has plummeted. When I was a kid, we talked about having flying cars and living to at least 100. Thank God we don't have flying cars. People hardly manage to get to the store and back on four wheels, never mind giving these people license to fly! The newspapers stopped reporting about life expectancy many years ago since it has come to a screeching halt if not gone backwards.

Take a look at all of the wrong in the world and how many people will fight with tooth and claw that it's all very "normal" and that we should legalize everything they want to do even when those things jeopardize our health, country, or the future of the human race.

Things are illegal for good reason, but there they go erasing the line of ethical behavior, redrawing it further and further back from logic and reason, decency and fairness, to the pits of insanity, degradation, and self-destruction.

"We want 64-ounce soda pop cups! Let's march on Capitol Hill! Let's boycott Hostess because they stopped making Twinkies! All honest people shouldn't be allowed to bear arms! Everything should be free of charge! Let's legalize all drugs."

I'd better stop now before I really get offensive ... as if I give a rat's ass about someone who wants to burn the Constitution or take away our human rights and personal freedoms all in the name of a "better world".

Dare to be Different

What can you do about the problem of the way things are? Not a whole hell of a lot; at least not overnight anyway. But you, for yourself, have options. You can be different, and you can positively affect the people in your proximity.

That's about the most important thing I can share with you. It may sound incredibly dumb or overly simple, but I'll be damned if the happiest, healthiest, most stable and even wealthiest individuals in the world behave nothing like the majority. In fact, they're ridiculed, called "eccentric" and even hated by "the crowd".

"The world is a funny place, and most people who live in it are clowns."—Anonymous

I didn't include this as an insult—well, maybe a little, but it's mainly to make a point. Living life, running a business, raising a family … whatever it is that you want to do well with, it's damn hard to make things go the way you want them to. And if you do what most people want, you're going to have a rough time of it.

Don't Think Like Most People

Most people think that nothing is possible, or worse, "they know everything" but haven't achieved a single thing. Yet, they're willing to tell you "the right way" to do things. To top it off, they make you wrong if you don't conform to their ways. You have to be hardened to the verbal attacks of others. The ole "sticks and stones" saying has merit. In other words, don't pay much attention to what people call you. Whoever said, "You've got to have thick skin," was right. Don't let things bother you, don't take it personally, and just keep going forward with your plan.

It's Not Easy to be Different

It's not easy to be different. People in the deadbeat camp, once they see you're not in agreement with their sordid views, will say you're a bad person and back it up by saying you did things that never actually happened. They will actually be committing the crimes they say you're doing.

They do this because they have no other "talents" but to degrade, demean, and blame.

If you're in business, your competition will say that you do shoddy work, the materials you use are substandard, and your products are inferior. If you offer services, they'll tell everybody you're a fake and don't know what you're talking about. One way or another, they will twist every good deed you do into something bad. All the while they are doing these very things themselves.

They think what they do is normal. The liar thinks everyone lies. The thief thinks everybody steals. The drug addict thinks everyone takes drugs. The cheat thinks everybody else will cheat on them, so they had better do it first.

The Cheaters Versus the Doers

There are those who roll up their sleeves and would rather DO something to improve life as we know it, and there are those who only complain about what a bad job those who are trying are doing. There are those who make progress and those who stop it.

And if you decide to leave problems up to "others" to fix, by default, you're in the camp of destructive people who are okay with the ship going down as long as they don't have to lift a finger as we sink. The whole way down, they would do nothing but bitch about how shitty a job the bailers trying to save the ship are doing.

Then you have those who will break all the rules. They'll lie and cheat. They take drugs and disregard the laws of the land. They do the dumbest things you can imagine to jeopardize their well-being and future preservation, and they argue that it's the right way to be. They'll make up stories about you because you are, in their eyes, a direct threat to them and their agenda.

You have to ask yourself, *Why are honest people referred to in derogatory ways?* In my day, an honest person was called a "goody two shoes". Someone bringing up the unethical behavior of another was "a tattletale" or a "snitch". Someone crossing a picket line was a "scab". I have no idea what the majority calls upstanding, productive, multi-determined movers and shakers these days, but without a doubt, there are degrading names for every one of them.

12
MANIPULATION

I'm not bringing this up to discourage you. The complete opposite, I am trying to prepare you for the challenges of life.

Parts of this book may seem a bit gloomy to you, but it's only to set the stage for you to realize what can happen in a competitive environment and what people are capable of doing under certain circumstances. This doesn't say you shouldn't trust anyone. It's just important to be aware that you can't trust everyone.

Like when you don't expect anyone to walk in your house, you still lock your doors; it's just good business to know what is possible.

Would you rather go through life with bad information that's been fed to you by people who have only their own gain in sight, or would you be better off knowing what's really going on around you?

It's like walking onto a football field without ever seeing the sport or knowing the rules. You need to be prepared for what's about to happen.

It's only ignorance that can allow you to be blindsided and laid flat before you even know what hits you. But then it's too late. Those who have tricked you are calling the shots, and there's nothing you can do about it in that eleventh hour.

To walk up to a player to shake his hand after the ball has been hiked, unaware of his intention of mauling you over, you're dead meat. But if you understand this person wants to take your head off and get to the quarterback and take *his* head off, you just might act a little differently and help your team win the game. Or at least be *prepared for the potential* of being knocked on your ass.

Like I said, the world is a tough place to live and succeed, so it's better to be prepared than vulnerable.

In reality, all of this would be perfectly fine if everyone were fair and honest. Most of us *do* play a fair game. The sad thing is, we start out with the gullible misconception that everybody else is honest and fair too, though some individuals refuse to play by the rules.

And that's something to be aware of. Those who can't do things very well believe they have no other option but to cheat. The right thing to do would be to hunker down to learn and get better at what they do. But for whatever reason, this logical approach doesn't cross their minds.

The one thing everyone can agree on, no matter what camp they're in or beliefs they hold, is that no one wants to be a sucker. No one likes to be lied to or tricked into things they weren't aware they were getting into with biased information and alteration of facts. And the one thing that would destroy the smoke and mirrors of the underlying establishment is the revelation that some people lie.

If you understand that people are *capable* of cheating and lying, and some people only do things dishonestly, then you are prepared for the times it happens. You may be fooled once, but you won't keep coming back for more abuse.

Life would be terrible if we looked at everyone as a liar. That would be too far-reaching and unfair to honest people, of which there are many. The only solution I've ever had is to give everyone a chance. The opportunity is theirs to lose by breaking the bond of trust.

In my day, one's word and handshake was more binding than anything. A guy would rather die than go back on his word. Today, this isn't the way it is. If you don't have your arrangements and agreements in writing, even notarized, you're screwed if some fall out were to happen. When it comes to a point of verbal claims being thrown around, the only way to protect yourself is with physical proof—documentation—and even then, you can have a hard time of it. But written agreements with signatures go a lot further than verbal claims. Things can go along nicely for months or even years, but when something goes wrong, that "nice" person can suddenly become ruthless and pretty evil, making up lies and doing whatever harm they can. You really don't know someone until you see them when things go wrong. That's when you see what they are capable of.

We could get into who and why, but that's not as important as how to recognize when you're being fed a bunch of bull. The first step in recognizing a lie, which also reveals the liar, is to verify the claims with *your own* inspection. There are too many opinions and not enough facts rushing around to just take someone's "studied" and "scholarly" words as fact. No one should have that much power over others, and yet that's all we see today—opinions gilded with claims of it all being fact.

It's hard to believe by good people that individuals can do things unfairly. Some will lie through their teeth as they look you in the eye with zero regard for how harmful their lies are to countless people. That's just the way it is. That's why you can't try to please everybody. You could be undertaking one of the kindest, most admirable ventures of the century, and there would still be people who hate what you're doing.

Here's the point: *you cannot be fooled if you understand the extent to which some individuals will go for their own benefit.*

You can't let yourself be tricked into supporting something you don't want because what you want is too important to abandon.

Another point that supersedes all others is: *the only way you can be swindled is to not make your own investigation.*

If you listen to the rumors or the "expert opinions" of others without your own verification to at least *some* of what they say, you can be manipulated. You have to make your own personal observation of the *actual* things, not the words or videos taken out of context. If it seems to stink, then you investigate more about that person or situation.

Don't take what I say in this book as gospel, but instead take this information and *see for yourself* whether it has merit or not. Don't listen, observe. You can't watch the news and say that you've done your homework. You have to actually look at the real thing to know what's going on. It's best to watch a live event because things can only be twisted after the fact with words.

13
ENTITLEMENT HAS KILLED MOTIVATION

"Bull" by Any Other Name

Our young, impressionable minds are being persuaded in colleges and universities that everybody should be handed an even piece of the pie even though they didn't work for it. They are convinced that big government should take care of them and that they are entitled, and everything should be free. Yet hundreds of years has shown this to be fantasy. They are delusional. They squash any free speech on campuses in order to stop any possibility of these bright kids making up their own minds about how they should live their lives.

Maybe it's promoted because of how appealing a "perfect" world might be. With that appeal, they can get an entire generation to follow them to the ends of the earth. Just remember that fairy tales were written to sell books, dolls, wedding dresses and amusement park tickets. Nothing wrong with them; it's okay to dream, but they are just not real. "Perfect" doesn't exist in the real world. It's really the difference between being practical with a plan and wishful thinking with no plan on how to create something that works.

They also push on the heartstrings of our youth in how cruel and heartless the capitalist is. And yet it is the hard-working entrepreneur who gives back to their communities and the world.

How do you talk to someone who is not in touch with reality? You don't. They just want to argue anyway, especially when they see you as cruel and heartless. You just get to work creating your life the best way possible. From there, you will then be able to help more people and do your part to make a better world.

No Accountability, Entitlement, and the "I Deserve It" Generation— The Perfect Storm

As I mentioned earlier, I recently spoke to a sports coach for a school in Illinois, and he told me that there is a mandate that requires all coaches to let every kid have equal time playing, even if they don't show up for practice!

Contrary to the popular opinion, getting a trophy for participation and all of this other BS is one of the meanest things our generation could have possibly done to our kids. Whether done as a calculated scheme to turn our society into a bunch of unambitious slugs or just plain ignorance, one of the few places where kids can be challenged today and learn that greatness comes out of working hard and striving for something is in sports.

What's so sickening about this is that as soon as these kids graduate and enter the real world, they're not going to be prepared. They're going to be disillusioned that everybody should give them what they want without earning it.

They're going to think that life needs to give them a job, and their boss needs to pay them whether they come to work or not. They should receive pay raises whether they do a good job or not. They get to have do-overs, and people should have pity on them and be understanding why they can't pay the rent. They're going to be out on their asses faster than you can say, "Life doesn't care about your excuses no matter how legitimate they might be."

Society has been driven down to the point of not wanting to work. There's no pride for what we do anymore. But that's the majority and probably always has been. Before you lose all hope, realize that there is the less popular way of pursuing life, business, success and happiness.

That's right, there is a rare, large group of people, though small in comparison to the norm, who are making a killing in business and doing great in life.

The fact is, success has always been a rare thing. Just look at how few millionaires and billionaires there are in comparison to the almost eight billion people on the planet, and it has gotten a lot worse.

What does this mean to you? Well, one of two things:

1. You join the majority of self-centered complainers who want handouts and the government to take care of them, or

2. You join the ranks of the hard-working people who have a purpose in life that goes beyond just themselves.

Without question, the first choice will leave you bitter and miserable. You'll be jealous of the people who think for themselves and walk with their heads held high, with satisfied grins.

The second one will leave you with the feeling of pride. You're allowed to contribute to society by offering products or services that people have a need for. You'll be able to stand on your own two feet and be self-reliant, not needy for state support or only living with the basic necessities, paycheck to paycheck.

And here's what's really incredible...

Option 2 has never been more favorable than right now. Why? Because so many more people of the majority don't want to work. The poor bastards who try to work without doing are the ones who fail in business within the first three years.

Much of the competition today are just going through the motions. They want success without the sweat. They expect people to show up at their door and throw money at them when in fact no one even knows they are in business or where they're located because they're too lazy to promote.

When Not to Help Your Child

One of the Hardest Things to do as a Parent is to Not Help Them.

As parents, we start out 100% helping our children. They're totally reliant on us for survival. But there's an interesting phenomenon about raising a child:

A Gradient of Responsibility Needs to be Granted Children as They Grow.

A good parent isn't defined as one who gives a lot of possessions or money. Today, most people think this is parenting, but it's not.

Kids need to be able to grow in the sense of thinking, making decisions, solving problems, and becoming more independent. But when we keep deciding for them, solving their little problems (that are big to them), we deprive them of the necessary preparation for life when they go out on their own.

Under your watchful eye and protection of the homestead, children are able to face trial and error without much danger. The lessons of life don't begin at age eighteen. They begin at the development ages: crawling, walking, learning to speak, learning to get along with other kids. They begin to learn about how they can give back to the family for all they receive.

The first time you see your child struggle and become frustrated about fitting a block into the right opening is painful to watch. Every fiber of your being wants to take the block and put it in the square hole for them. But each time we do that, they lose their opportunity to become independent and capable. Of course, you can and should show them, but don't take over and do it for them.

Allow Your Kids a Progressive Process of Independence

Too many times, I've watched parents look for jobs for their kids. They wanted their child to be productive and so on. That's great, but I could see the humiliation on the boy's face when mommy and daddy, still treating their kid like a totally dependent newborn, came in to my company asking if I would hire their kid for the summer.

These parents were still holding their kid's hands, and they'd been doing it their entire lives! The kid was never given the gradient of independence he so definitely needed.

A friend taught me that if a parent calls asking you to hire their son or daughter, don't hire them because the kid will do everything in their power to get fired. They didn't want the job. On the other hand, when a kid walks in on their own volition, hire them.

I taught my boys as best I could what I knew, but we as humans don't accept other people's teachings until we need it. We always think, *I got this*. It's when our kids fail that they become more willing to heed your advice. So give it generously—a little with each opportunity to share your experience—and they will hear your voice when what they thought was the way to do something goes bust.

Other times, they will be right, but either way, success or failure, they learn what works in their lives.

14

CONCLUSION
OPEN YOUR EARS

Learn something new every day. There are many ways to learn, but this can be done as simply as observing what goes on around you and asking yourself, "OK, what can I learn from this?"

No doubt, you will learn the most in the shortest period of time by having a mentor or two who have already achieved what you want to make happen. You surround yourself with smart people and pay them well, which includes mentors. What you learn might be something that you don't want to do. It could be something very easy or not so easy. One of the hardest things to do is shut your trap and open your ears. Everyone you talk to, you learn something from them. It might be, "Don't do that!" and you have to be willing to listen and receive criticism. You don't want to come off as the guy who knows everything. I am pretty good at keeping my mouth shut. When I see there is a lesson to be learned with someone I am working with, I don't say, "I told you so." I give a nod instead to give attention to the point.

Opportunity

There is a ton of opportunity out there. You can take it and run with it, especially in a menial job. Just because you get your hands dirty doesn't mean you are stupid.

Keep Your Mouth Shut

Be a stealth person. Don't be a flash or else others will copy you and do it out of their garage and be in direct competition with you. My common thing to say is, "We're doing okay," when asked. Drive it, live it … and the cat's out of the bag.

Success and Profit

Being successful in business is not as easy as it looks. In business, there are a lot of hidden costs that just making a profit requires a lot of knowledge and skill.

Keep it Real

We had a little makeup mirror with a handle hanging on the wall in our bathroom. That was our vanity. I remember standing there looking into the mirror and wondering "What did I do? What did I get myself involved in?" That mirror is still in my desk drawer today. Whenever I start to think that I'm better than others, have a big head, I'm really something … I pull the mirror out and look at it, and my feet hit the ground again. It reminds me where I came from.

Struggle Through to Get it Done

We didn't have any dough to afford the equipment we needed in the beginning, so we had to do things the hard way—by hand. It was not fun, but we did what we had to in order to get things done and survive. Keeping the early days in mind helps to keep you grounded and brings you back to where you came from, like I have with the mirror in my drawer.

You have an incredible opportunity to be extremely successful just by having good work ethic. Add the advantage of the mentorship this book shares with you, and you're going to be unstoppable.

You have a huge advantage! Don't miss this opportunity to live a rewarding life.